ON YOUR 50TH
Birthday!

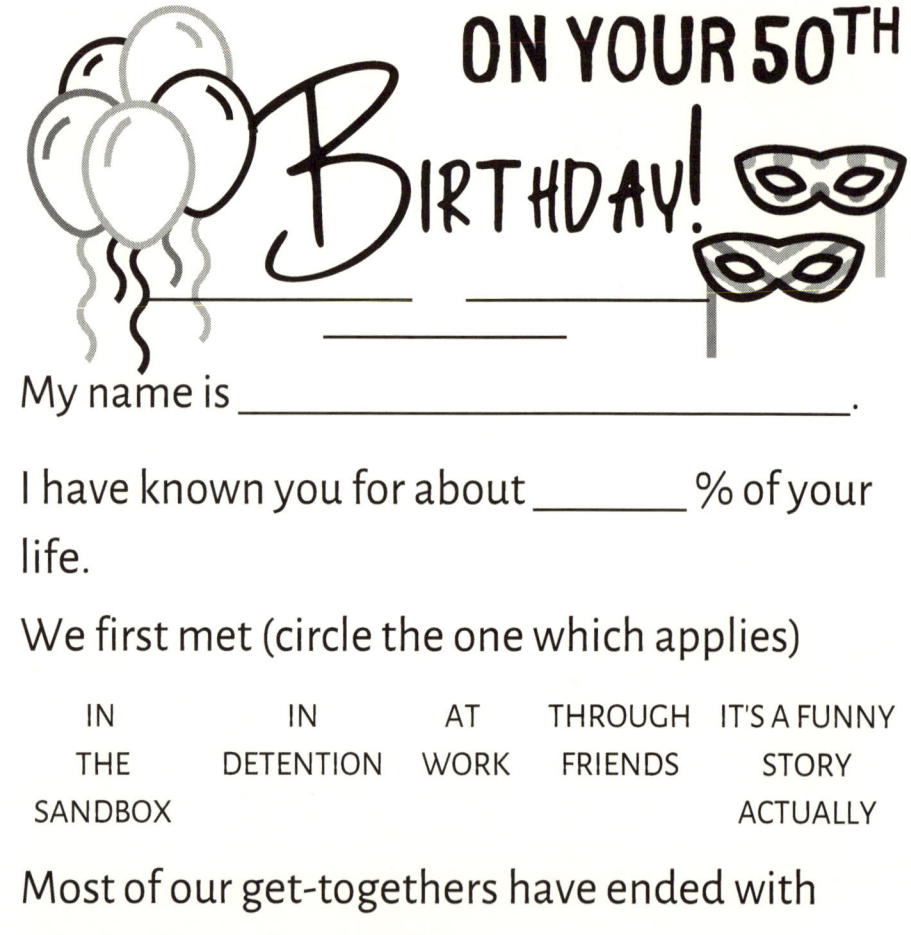

ON YOUR 50TH BIRTHDAY!

My name is _____.

I have known you for about _____ % of your life.

We first met (circle the one which applies)

   IN THE SANDBOX   IN DETENTION   AT WORK   THROUGH FRIENDS   IT'S A FUNNY STORY ACTUALLY

Most of our get-togethers have ended with (circle those that apply)

   TEARS OF LAUGHTER   EMPTY BANK ACCOUNTS   TRIPS TO THE E.R   BLACKOUTS

Remember that time when we

_____

_____

My birthday wish for you is _____

_____

ON YOUR 50TH BIRTHDAY!

My name is _____.

I have known you for about _____ % of your life.

We first met (circle the one which applies)

    IN THE SANDBOX   IN DETENTION   AT WORK   THROUGH FRIENDS   IT'S A FUNNY STORY ACTUALLY

Most of our get-togethers have ended with (circle those that apply)

    TEARS OF LAUGHTER   EMPTY BANK ACCOUNTS   TRIPS TO THE E.R   BLACKOUTS

Remember that time when we
_____
_____

My birthday wish for you is _____
_____.

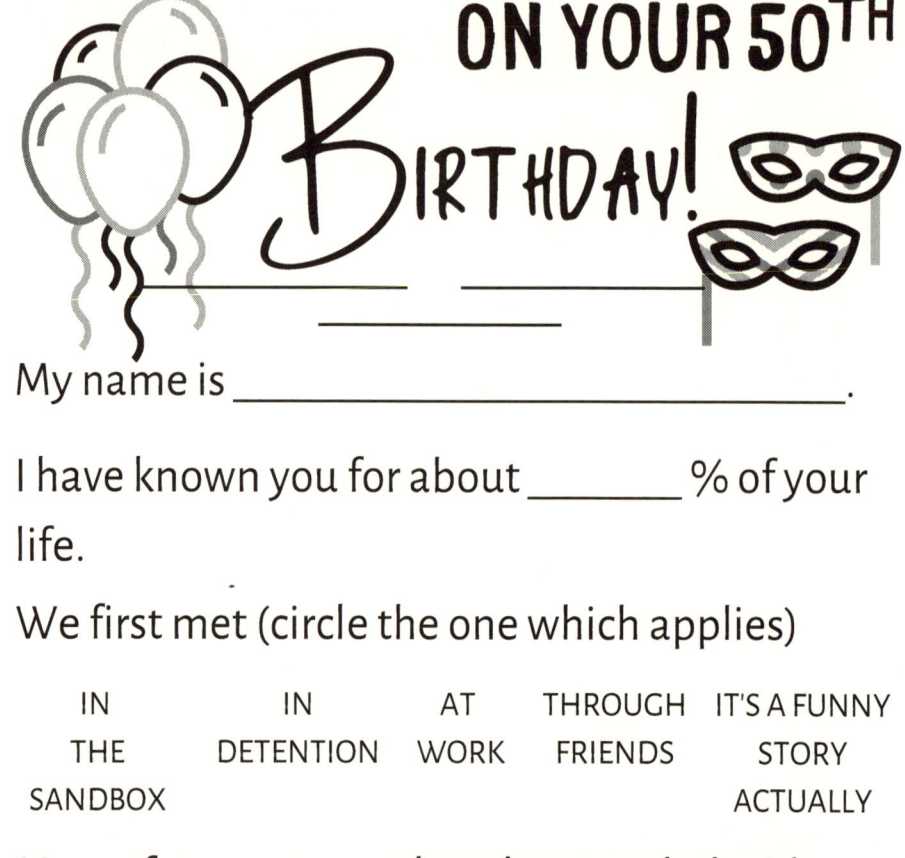

ON YOUR 50TH Birthday!

My name is _____.

I have known you for about _____ % of your life.

We first met (circle the one which applies)

   IN THE SANDBOX   IN DETENTION   AT WORK   THROUGH FRIENDS   IT'S A FUNNY STORY ACTUALLY

Most of our get-togethers have ended with (circle those that apply)

   TEARS OF LAUGHTER   EMPTY BANK ACCOUNTS   TRIPS TO THE E.R   BLACKOUTS

Remember that time when we

_____

_____

My birthday wish for you is _____

_____.

ON YOUR 50TH Birthday!

My name is _____.

I have known you for about _____ % of your life.

We first met (circle the one which applies)

   IN THE SANDBOX   IN DETENTION   AT WORK   THROUGH FRIENDS   IT'S A FUNNY STORY ACTUALLY

Most of our get-togethers have ended with (circle those that apply)

   TEARS OF LAUGHTER   EMPTY BANK ACCOUNTS   TRIPS TO THE E.R   BLACKOUTS

Remember that time when we

_____

_____

My birthday wish for you is _____

_____.

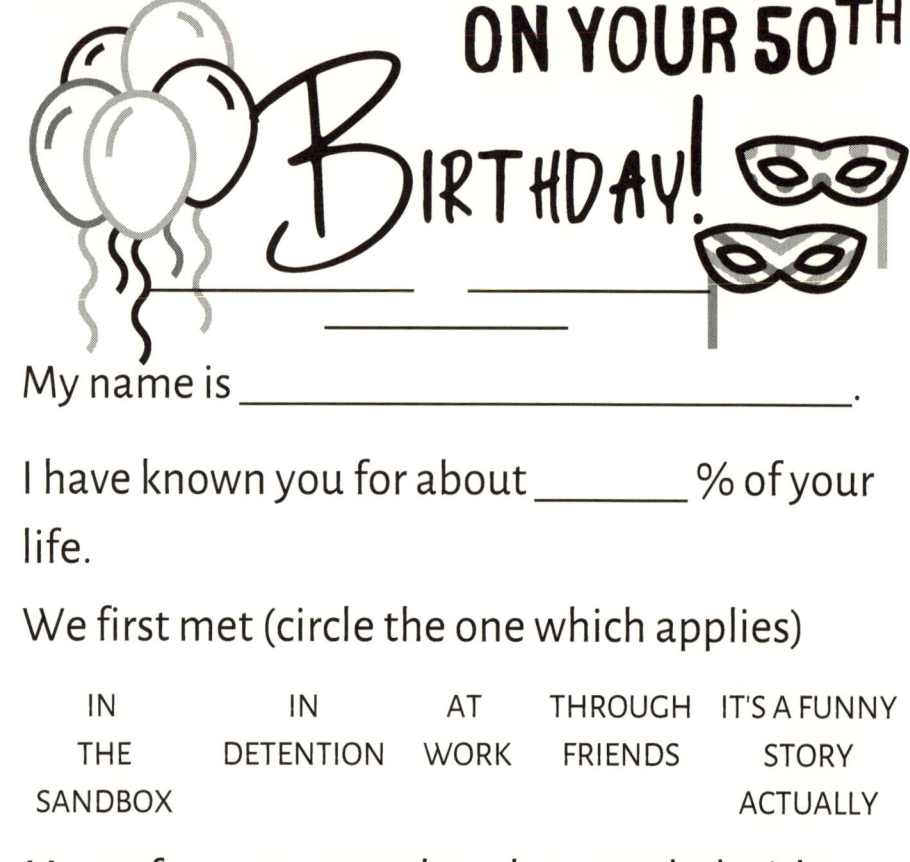

ON YOUR 50TH Birthday!

My name is _____.

I have known you for about _____ % of your life.

We first met (circle the one which applies)

| IN THE SANDBOX | IN DETENTION | AT WORK | THROUGH FRIENDS | IT'S A FUNNY STORY ACTUALLY |

Most of our get-togethers have ended with (circle those that apply)

| TEARS OF LAUGHTER | EMPTY BANK ACCOUNTS | TRIPS TO THE E.R | BLACKOUTS |

Remember that time when we

_____

_____

My birthday wish for you is _____

_____.

My name is _____.

I have known you for about _____ % of your life.

We first met (circle the one which applies)

| IN THE SANDBOX | IN DETENTION | AT WORK | THROUGH FRIENDS | IT'S A FUNNY STORY ACTUALLY |

Most of our get-togethers have ended with (circle those that apply)

| TEARS OF LAUGHTER | EMPTY BANK ACCOUNTS | TRIPS TO THE E.R | BLACKOUTS |

Remember that time when we

_____
_____

My birthday wish for you is _____
_____.

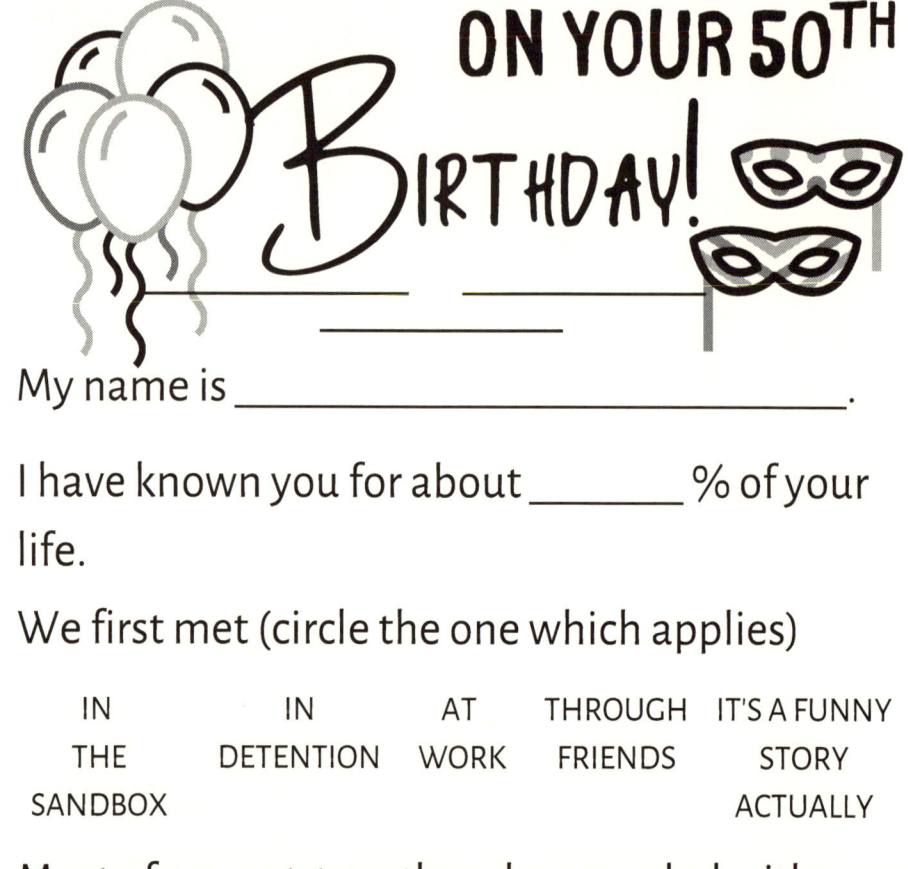

ON YOUR 50TH Birthday!

My name is _____.

I have known you for about _____ % of your life.

We first met (circle the one which applies)

IN THE SANDBOX   IN DETENTION   AT WORK   THROUGH FRIENDS   IT'S A FUNNY STORY ACTUALLY

Most of our get-togethers have ended with (circle those that apply)

TEARS OF LAUGHTER   EMPTY BANK ACCOUNTS   TRIPS TO THE E.R   BLACKOUTS

Remember that time when we
_____
_____

My birthday wish for you is _____
_____.

ON YOUR 50TH Birthday!

My name is _____.

I have known you for about _____ % of your life.

We first met (circle the one which applies)

| IN THE SANDBOX | IN DETENTION | AT WORK | THROUGH FRIENDS | IT'S A FUNNY STORY ACTUALLY |

Most of our get-togethers have ended with (circle those that apply)

| TEARS OF LAUGHTER | EMPTY BANK ACCOUNTS | TRIPS TO THE E.R | BLACKOUTS |

Remember that time when we

_____

_____

My birthday wish for you is _____

_____.

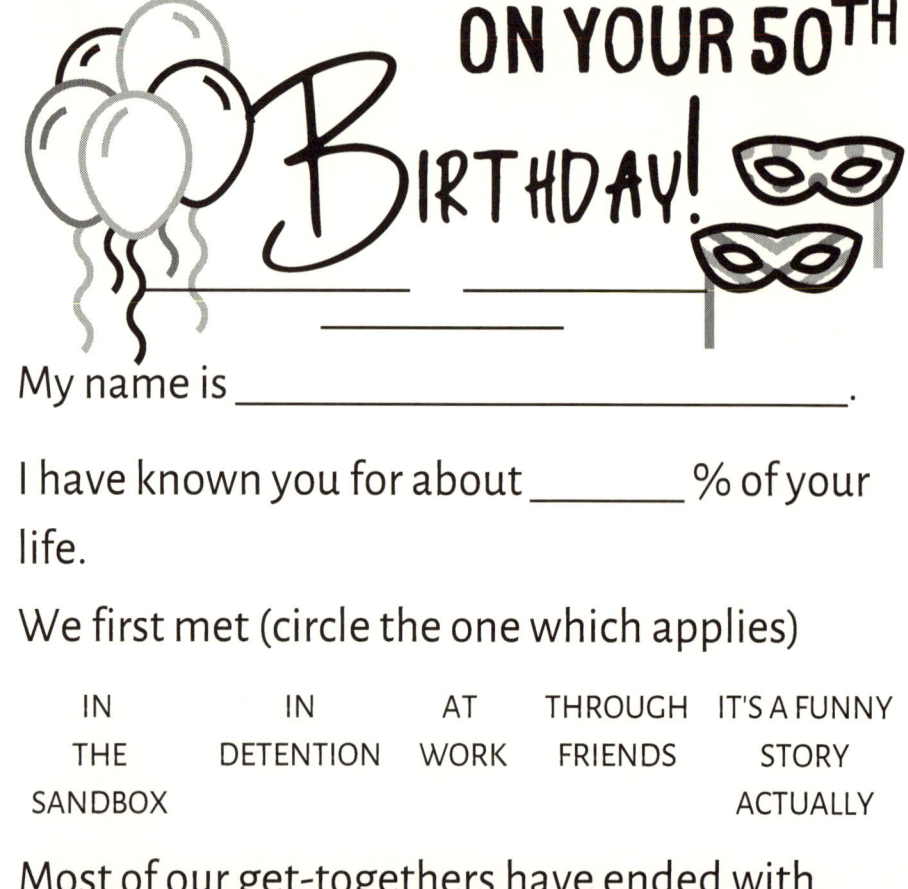

ON YOUR 50TH Birthday!

My name is _____.

I have known you for about _____ % of your life.

We first met (circle the one which applies)

| IN THE SANDBOX | IN DETENTION | AT WORK | THROUGH FRIENDS | IT'S A FUNNY STORY ACTUALLY |

Most of our get-togethers have ended with (circle those that apply)

| TEARS OF LAUGHTER | EMPTY BANK ACCOUNTS | TRIPS TO THE E.R | BLACKOUTS |

Remember that time when we
_____
_____

My birthday wish for you is _____
_____.

ON YOUR 50TH Birthday!

_____ _____

My name is _____.

I have known you for about _____ % of your life.

We first met (circle the one which applies)

   IN THE SANDBOX   IN DETENTION   AT WORK   THROUGH FRIENDS   IT'S A FUNNY STORY ACTUALLY

Most of our get-togethers have ended with (circle those that apply)

   TEARS OF LAUGHTER   EMPTY BANK ACCOUNTS   TRIPS TO THE E.R   BLACKOUTS

Remember that time when we

_____

_____

My birthday wish for you is _____

_____.

ON YOUR 50TH Birthday!

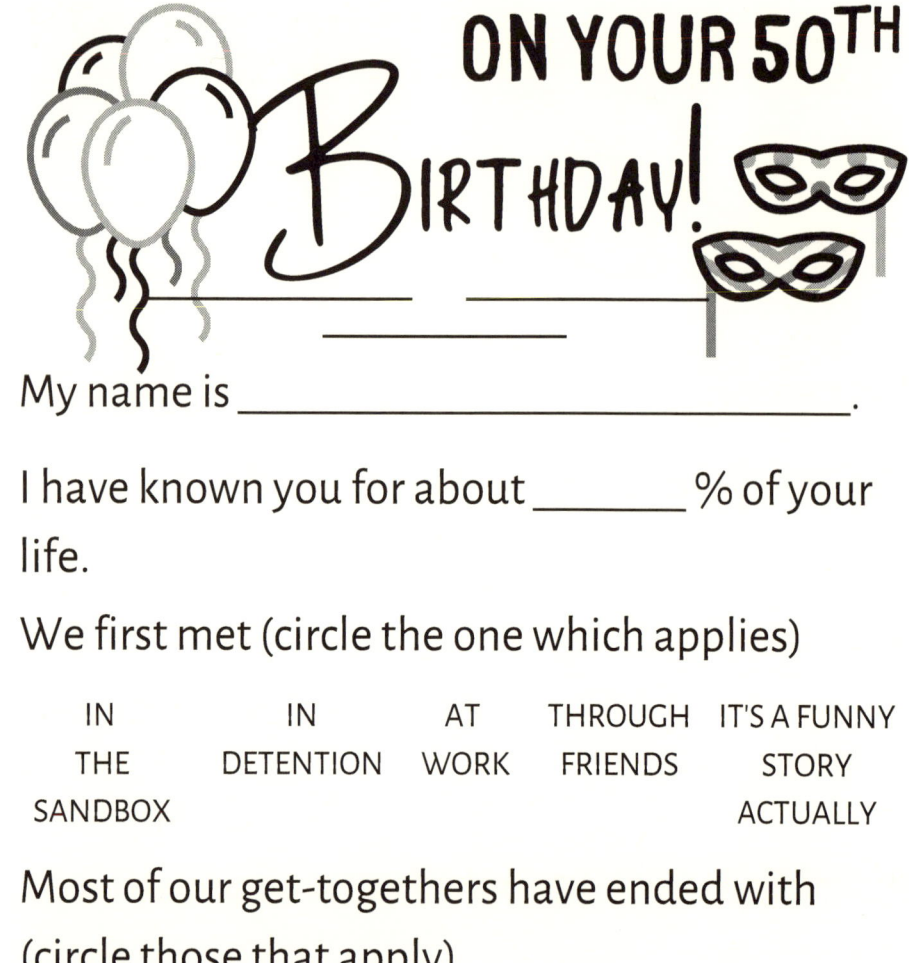

My name is _____.

I have known you for about _____ % of your life.

We first met (circle the one which applies)

| IN THE SANDBOX | IN DETENTION | AT WORK | THROUGH FRIENDS | IT'S A FUNNY STORY ACTUALLY |

Most of our get-togethers have ended with (circle those that apply)

| TEARS OF LAUGHTER | EMPTY BANK ACCOUNTS | TRIPS TO THE E.R | BLACKOUTS |

Remember that time when we

_____

_____

My birthday wish for you is _____

_____.

ON YOUR 50TH BIRTHDAY!

_____ _____
      _____

My name is _____.

I have known you for about _____ % of your life.

We first met (circle the one which applies)

   IN THE SANDBOX   IN DETENTION   AT WORK   THROUGH FRIENDS   IT'S A FUNNY STORY ACTUALLY

Most of our get-togethers have ended with (circle those that apply)

   TEARS OF LAUGHTER   EMPTY BANK ACCOUNTS   TRIPS TO THE E.R   BLACKOUTS

Remember that time when we

_____

_____

My birthday wish for you is _____

_____.

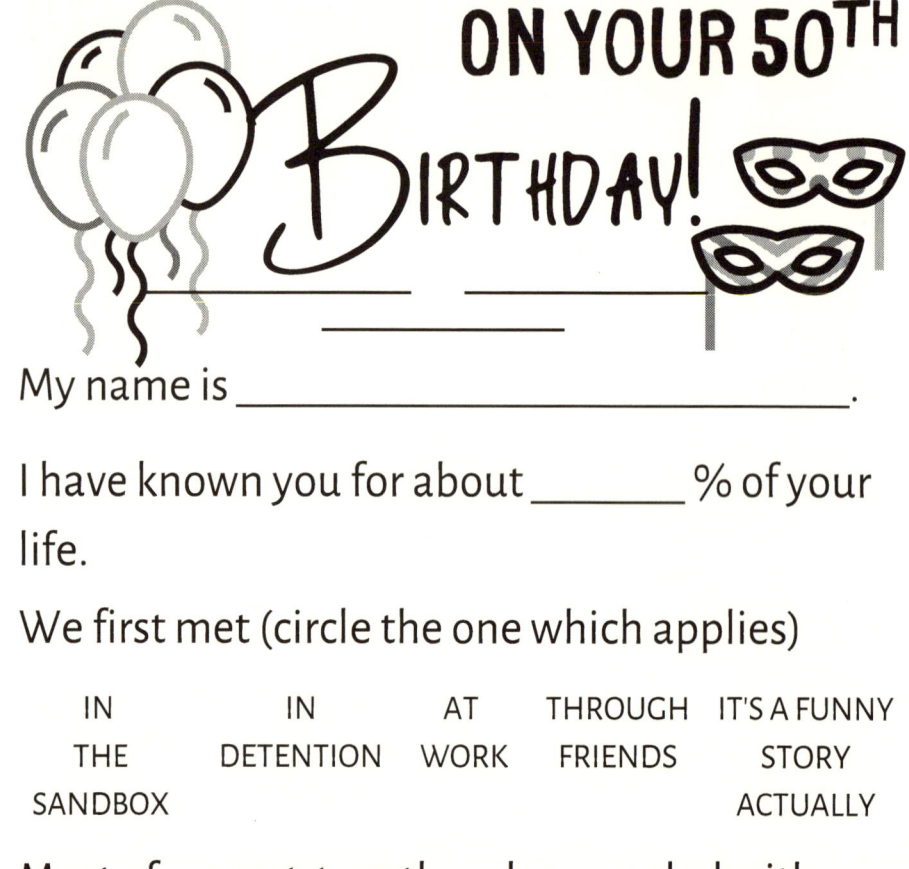

ON YOUR 50TH BIRTHDAY!

My name is _____.

I have known you for about _____ % of your life.

We first met (circle the one which applies)

   IN THE SANDBOX   IN DETENTION   AT WORK   THROUGH FRIENDS   IT'S A FUNNY STORY ACTUALLY

Most of our get-togethers have ended with (circle those that apply)

   TEARS OF LAUGHTER   EMPTY BANK ACCOUNTS   TRIPS TO THE E.R   BLACKOUTS

Remember that time when we

_____

_____

My birthday wish for you is _____

_____

My name is _____.

I have known you for about _____ % of your life.

We first met (circle the one which applies)

IN THE SANDBOX   IN DETENTION   AT WORK   THROUGH FRIENDS   IT'S A FUNNY STORY ACTUALLY

Most of our get-togethers have ended with (circle those that apply)

TEARS OF LAUGHTER   EMPTY BANK ACCOUNTS   TRIPS TO THE E.R   BLACKOUTS

Remember that time when we
_____
_____

My birthday wish for you is _____
_____.

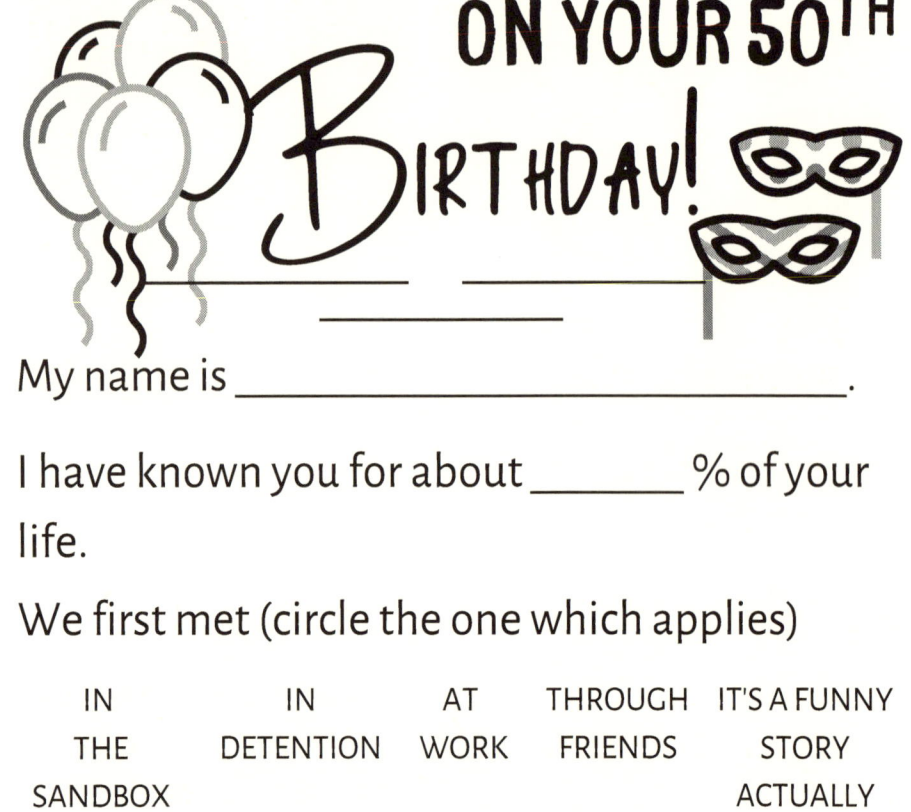

ON YOUR 50TH Birthday!

My name is _____.

I have known you for about _____ % of your life.

We first met (circle the one which applies)

| IN THE SANDBOX | IN DETENTION | AT WORK | THROUGH FRIENDS | IT'S A FUNNY STORY ACTUALLY |

Most of our get-togethers have ended with (circle those that apply)

| TEARS OF LAUGHTER | EMPTY BANK ACCOUNTS | TRIPS TO THE E.R | BLACKOUTS |

Remember that time when we
_____
_____

My birthday wish for you is _____
_____.

ON YOUR 50TH BIRTHDAY!

My name is _____.

I have known you for about _____ % of your life.

We first met (circle the one which applies)

    IN THE SANDBOX   IN DETENTION   AT WORK   THROUGH FRIENDS   IT'S A FUNNY STORY ACTUALLY

Most of our get-togethers have ended with (circle those that apply)

    TEARS OF LAUGHTER   EMPTY BANK ACCOUNTS   TRIPS TO THE E.R   BLACKOUTS

Remember that time when we
_____
_____

My birthday wish for you is _____
_____.

ON YOUR 50TH Birthday!

_____ _____

My name is _____.

I have known you for about _____ % of your life.

We first met (circle the one which applies)

IN THE SANDBOX   IN DETENTION   AT WORK   THROUGH FRIENDS   IT'S A FUNNY STORY ACTUALLY

Most of our get-togethers have ended with (circle those that apply)

TEARS OF LAUGHTER   EMPTY BANK ACCOUNTS   TRIPS TO THE E.R   BLACKOUTS

Remember that time when we
_____
_____

My birthday wish for you is _____
_____.

ON YOUR 50TH Birthday!

My name is _____.

I have known you for about _____ % of your life.

We first met (circle the one which applies)

   IN THE SANDBOX   IN DETENTION   AT WORK   THROUGH FRIENDS   IT'S A FUNNY STORY ACTUALLY

Most of our get-togethers have ended with (circle those that apply)

   TEARS OF LAUGHTER   EMPTY BANK ACCOUNTS   TRIPS TO THE E.R   BLACKOUTS

Remember that time when we

_____

_____

My birthday wish for you is _____

_____.

ON YOUR 50TH BIRTHDAY!

My name is _____.

I have known you for about _____ % of your life.

We first met (circle the one which applies)

   IN THE SANDBOX   IN DETENTION   AT WORK   THROUGH FRIENDS   IT'S A FUNNY STORY ACTUALLY

Most of our get-togethers have ended with (circle those that apply)

   TEARS OF LAUGHTER   EMPTY BANK ACCOUNTS   TRIPS TO THE E.R   BLACKOUTS

Remember that time when we

_____

_____

My birthday wish for you is _____

_____

ON YOUR 50TH Birthday!

My name is _____.

I have known you for about _____ % of your life.

We first met (circle the one which applies)

IN THE SANDBOX   IN DETENTION   AT WORK   THROUGH FRIENDS   IT'S A FUNNY STORY ACTUALLY

Most of our get-togethers have ended with (circle those that apply)

TEARS OF LAUGHTER   EMPTY BANK ACCOUNTS   TRIPS TO THE E.R   BLACKOUTS

Remember that time when we
_____
_____

My birthday wish for you is _____
_____.

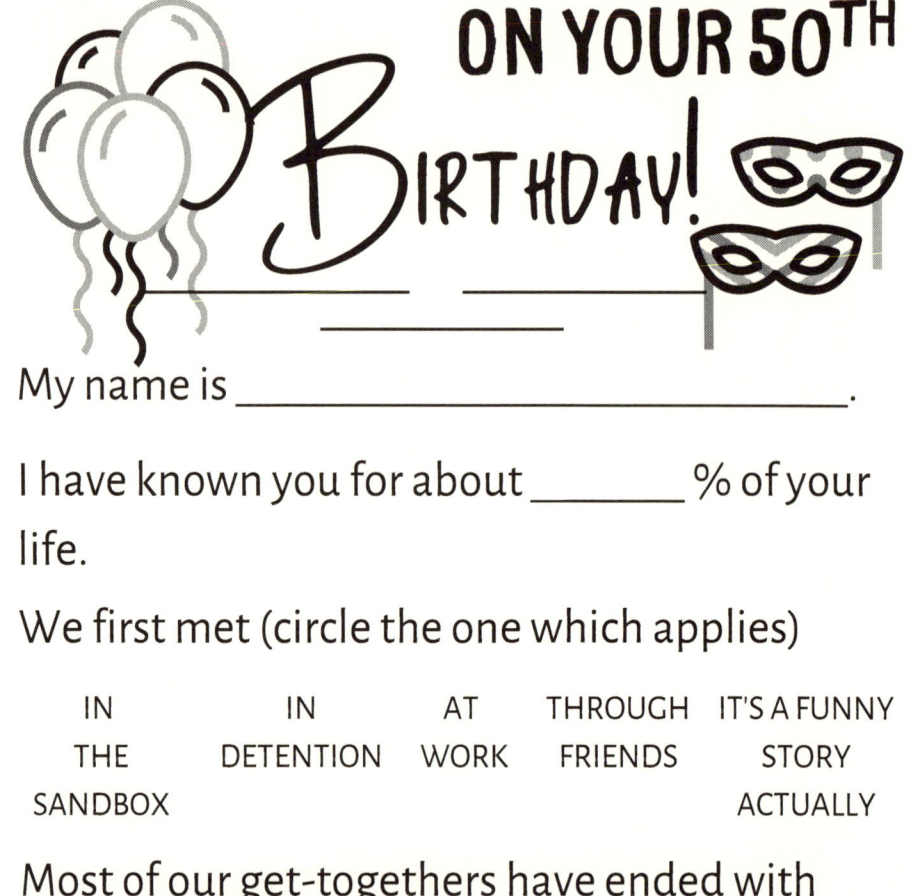

ON YOUR 50TH Birthday!

_____   _____

My name is _____.

I have known you for about _____ % of your life.

We first met (circle the one which applies)

   IN THE SANDBOX   IN DETENTION   AT WORK   THROUGH FRIENDS   IT'S A FUNNY STORY ACTUALLY

Most of our get-togethers have ended with (circle those that apply)

   TEARS OF LAUGHTER   EMPTY BANK ACCOUNTS   TRIPS TO THE E.R   BLACKOUTS

Remember that time when we

_____

_____

My birthday wish for you is _____

_____.

ON YOUR 50TH BIRTHDAY!

My name is _____.

I have known you for about _____ % of your life.

We first met (circle the one which applies)

    IN THE SANDBOX   IN DETENTION   AT WORK   THROUGH FRIENDS   IT'S A FUNNY STORY ACTUALLY

Most of our get-togethers have ended with (circle those that apply)

    TEARS OF LAUGHTER   EMPTY BANK ACCOUNTS   TRIPS TO THE E.R   BLACKOUTS

Remember that time when we

_____

_____

My birthday wish for you is _____

_____.

ON YOUR 50TH Birthday!

My name is _____.

I have known you for about _____ % of your life.

We first met (circle the one which applies)

   IN THE SANDBOX   IN DETENTION   AT WORK   THROUGH FRIENDS   IT'S A FUNNY STORY ACTUALLY

Most of our get-togethers have ended with (circle those that apply)

   TEARS OF LAUGHTER   EMPTY BANK ACCOUNTS   TRIPS TO THE E.R   BLACKOUTS

Remember that time when we

_____

_____

My birthday wish for you is _____

_____.

ON YOUR 50TH Birthday!

My name is _____.

I have known you for about _____ % of your life.

We first met (circle the one which applies)

   IN THE SANDBOX   IN DETENTION   AT WORK   THROUGH FRIENDS   IT'S A FUNNY STORY ACTUALLY

Most of our get-togethers have ended with (circle those that apply)

   TEARS OF LAUGHTER   EMPTY BANK ACCOUNTS   TRIPS TO THE E.R   BLACKOUTS

Remember that time when we

_____

_____

My birthday wish for you is _____

_____.

ON YOUR 50TH Birthday!

My name is _____.

I have known you for about _____ % of your life.

We first met (circle the one which applies)

   IN THE SANDBOX   IN DETENTION   AT WORK   THROUGH FRIENDS   IT'S A FUNNY STORY ACTUALLY

Most of our get-togethers have ended with (circle those that apply)

   TEARS OF LAUGHTER   EMPTY BANK ACCOUNTS   TRIPS TO THE E.R   BLACKOUTS

Remember that time when we

_____

_____

My birthday wish for you is _____

_____

ON YOUR 50TH Birthday!

_____ _____

My name is _____.

I have known you for about _____ % of your life.

We first met (circle the one which applies)

   IN THE SANDBOX   IN DETENTION   AT WORK   THROUGH FRIENDS   IT'S A FUNNY STORY ACTUALLY

Most of our get-togethers have ended with (circle those that apply)

   TEARS OF LAUGHTER   EMPTY BANK ACCOUNTS   TRIPS TO THE E.R   BLACKOUTS

Remember that time when we

_____

_____

My birthday wish for you is _____

_____.

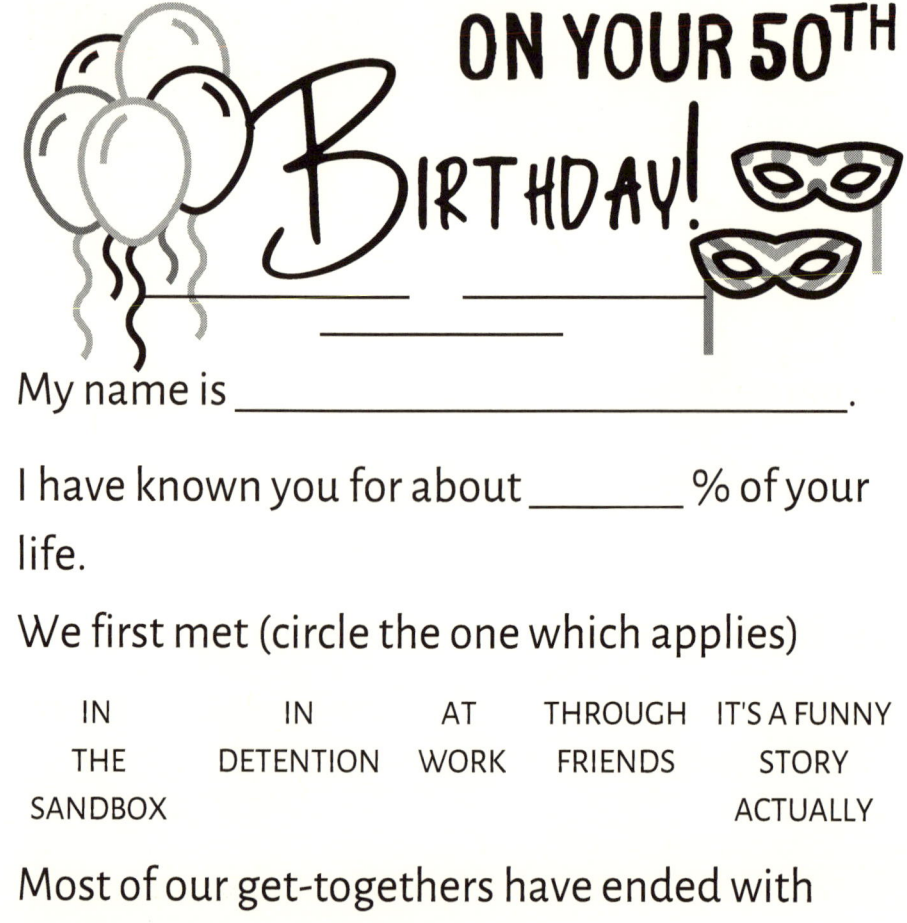

ON YOUR 50TH Birthday!

My name is _____.

I have known you for about _____ % of your life.

We first met (circle the one which applies)

   IN   IN   AT   THROUGH   IT'S A FUNNY
  THE   DETENTION   WORK   FRIENDS   STORY
SANDBOX   ACTUALLY

Most of our get-togethers have ended with (circle those that apply)

  TEARS OF   EMPTY BANK   TRIPS TO THE   BLACKOUTS
  LAUGHTER   ACCOUNTS   E.R

Remember that time when we

_____

_____

My birthday wish for you is _____

_____.

ON YOUR 50TH BIRTHDAY!

My name is _____.

I have known you for about _____ % of your life.

We first met (circle the one which applies)

| IN THE SANDBOX | IN DETENTION | AT WORK | THROUGH FRIENDS | IT'S A FUNNY STORY ACTUALLY |

Most of our get-togethers have ended with (circle those that apply)

| TEARS OF LAUGHTER | EMPTY BANK ACCOUNTS | TRIPS TO THE E.R | BLACKOUTS |

Remember that time when we
_____
_____

My birthday wish for you is _____
_____.

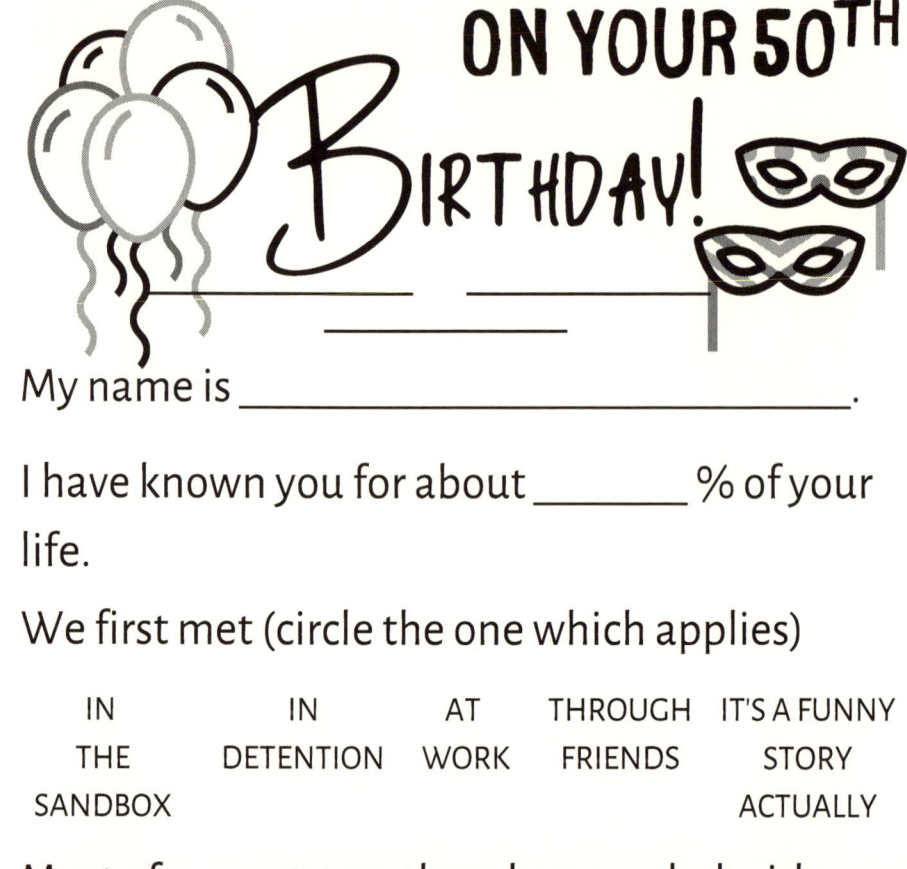

My name is _____.

I have known you for about _____ % of your life.

We first met (circle the one which applies)

   IN THE SANDBOX   IN DETENTION   AT WORK   THROUGH FRIENDS   IT'S A FUNNY STORY ACTUALLY

Most of our get-togethers have ended with (circle those that apply)

   TEARS OF LAUGHTER   EMPTY BANK ACCOUNTS   TRIPS TO THE E.R   BLACKOUTS

Remember that time when we

_____

_____

My birthday wish for you is _____

_____

ON YOUR 50TH Birthday!

My name is _____.

I have known you for about _____ % of your life.

We first met (circle the one which applies)

   IN THE SANDBOX   IN DETENTION   AT WORK   THROUGH FRIENDS   IT'S A FUNNY STORY ACTUALLY

Most of our get-togethers have ended with (circle those that apply)

   TEARS OF LAUGHTER   EMPTY BANK ACCOUNTS   TRIPS TO THE E.R   BLACKOUTS

Remember that time when we

_____

_____

My birthday wish for you is _____

_____.

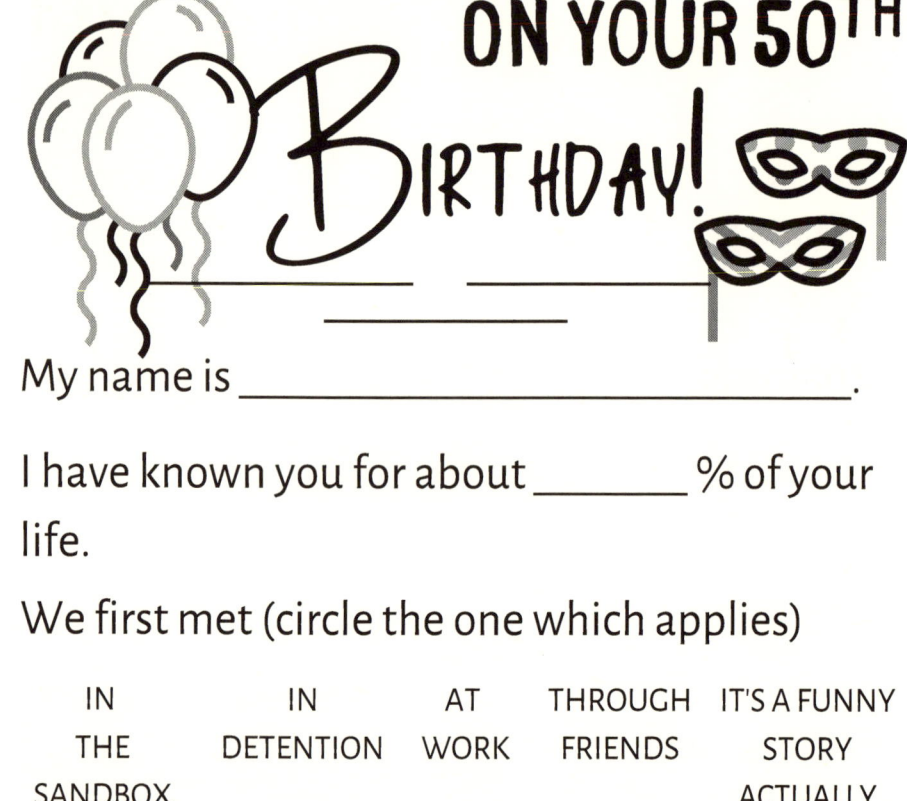

ON YOUR 50TH BIRTHDAY!

My name is _____.

I have known you for about _____ % of your life.

We first met (circle the one which applies)

   IN THE SANDBOX   IN DETENTION   AT WORK   THROUGH FRIENDS   IT'S A FUNNY STORY ACTUALLY

Most of our get-togethers have ended with (circle those that apply)

   TEARS OF LAUGHTER   EMPTY BANK ACCOUNTS   TRIPS TO THE E.R   BLACKOUTS

Remember that time when we

_____

_____

My birthday wish for you is _____

_____

ON YOUR 50TH BIRTHDAY!

My name is _____.

I have known you for about _____ % of your life.

We first met (circle the one which applies)

| IN THE SANDBOX | IN DETENTION | AT WORK | THROUGH FRIENDS | IT'S A FUNNY STORY ACTUALLY |

Most of our get-togethers have ended with (circle those that apply)

| TEARS OF LAUGHTER | EMPTY BANK ACCOUNTS | TRIPS TO THE E.R | BLACKOUTS |

Remember that time when we
_____
_____

My birthday wish for you is _____
_____.

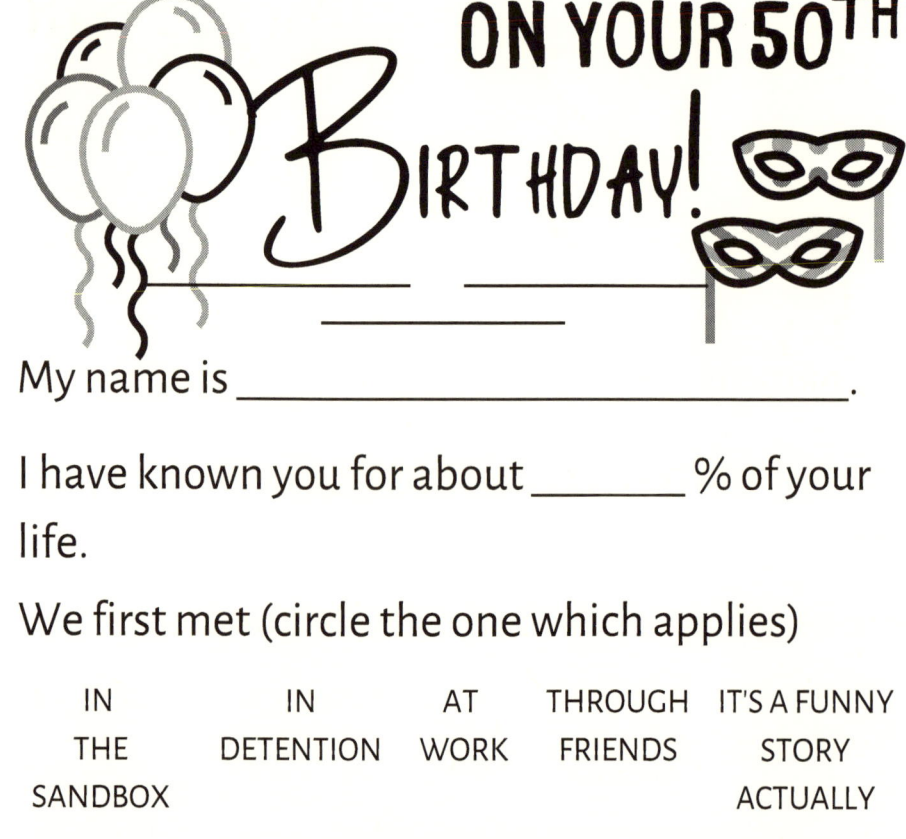

ON YOUR 50TH Birthday!

My name is _____.

I have known you for about _____ % of your life.

We first met (circle the one which applies)

   IN THE SANDBOX   IN DETENTION   AT WORK   THROUGH FRIENDS   IT'S A FUNNY STORY ACTUALLY

Most of our get-togethers have ended with (circle those that apply)

   TEARS OF LAUGHTER   EMPTY BANK ACCOUNTS   TRIPS TO THE E.R   BLACKOUTS

Remember that time when we

_____

_____

My birthday wish for you is _____

_____.

ON YOUR 50TH Birthday!

My name is _____.

I have known you for about _____ % of your life.

We first met (circle the one which applies)

| IN THE SANDBOX | IN DETENTION | AT WORK | THROUGH FRIENDS | IT'S A FUNNY STORY ACTUALLY |

Most of our get-togethers have ended with (circle those that apply)

| TEARS OF LAUGHTER | EMPTY BANK ACCOUNTS | TRIPS TO THE E.R | BLACKOUTS |

Remember that time when we
_____
_____

My birthday wish for you is _____
_____.

ON YOUR 50TH Birthday!

My name is _____.

I have known you for about _____ % of your life.

We first met (circle the one which applies)

   IN THE SANDBOX   IN DETENTION   AT WORK   THROUGH FRIENDS   IT'S A FUNNY STORY ACTUALLY

Most of our get-togethers have ended with (circle those that apply)

   TEARS OF LAUGHTER   EMPTY BANK ACCOUNTS   TRIPS TO THE E.R   BLACKOUTS

Remember that time when we

_____

_____

My birthday wish for you is _____

_____

ON YOUR 50TH BIRTHDAY!

My name is _____.

I have known you for about _____ % of your life.

We first met (circle the one which applies)

| IN THE SANDBOX | IN DETENTION | AT WORK | THROUGH FRIENDS | IT'S A FUNNY STORY ACTUALLY |

Most of our get-togethers have ended with (circle those that apply)

| TEARS OF LAUGHTER | EMPTY BANK ACCOUNTS | TRIPS TO THE E.R | BLACKOUTS |

Remember that time when we _____
_____

My birthday wish for you is _____
_____.

ON YOUR 50TH Birthday!

_____

My name is _____.

I have known you for about _____ % of your life.

We first met (circle the one which applies)

| IN THE SANDBOX | IN DETENTION | AT WORK | THROUGH FRIENDS | IT'S A FUNNY STORY ACTUALLY |

Most of our get-togethers have ended with (circle those that apply)

| TEARS OF LAUGHTER | EMPTY BANK ACCOUNTS | TRIPS TO THE E.R | BLACKOUTS |

Remember that time when we
_____
_____

My birthday wish for you is _____
_____

ON YOUR 50TH Birthday!

_____ _____

My name is _____.

I have known you for about _____ % of your life.

We first met (circle the one which applies)

| IN THE SANDBOX | IN DETENTION | AT WORK | THROUGH FRIENDS | IT'S A FUNNY STORY ACTUALLY |

Most of our get-togethers have ended with (circle those that apply)

| TEARS OF LAUGHTER | EMPTY BANK ACCOUNTS | TRIPS TO THE E.R | BLACKOUTS |

Remember that time when we

_____

_____

My birthday wish for you is _____

_____.

ON YOUR 50TH Birthday!

_____ _____

My name is _____.

I have known you for about _____ % of your life.

We first met (circle the one which applies)

    IN THE SANDBOX   IN DETENTION   AT WORK   THROUGH FRIENDS   IT'S A FUNNY STORY ACTUALLY

Most of our get-togethers have ended with (circle those that apply)

    TEARS OF LAUGHTER   EMPTY BANK ACCOUNTS   TRIPS TO THE E.R   BLACKOUTS

Remember that time when we

_____

_____

My birthday wish for you is _____

_____

ON YOUR 50TH BIRTHDAY!

My name is _____.

I have known you for about _____ % of your life.

We first met (circle the one which applies)

| IN THE SANDBOX | IN DETENTION | AT WORK | THROUGH FRIENDS | IT'S A FUNNY STORY ACTUALLY |

Most of our get-togethers have ended with (circle those that apply)

| TEARS OF LAUGHTER | EMPTY BANK ACCOUNTS | TRIPS TO THE E.R | BLACKOUTS |

Remember that time when we
_____
_____

My birthday wish for you is _____
_____.

ON YOUR 50TH Birthday!

_____ _____

My name is _____.

I have known you for about _____ % of your life.

We first met (circle the one which applies)

| IN THE SANDBOX | IN DETENTION | AT WORK | THROUGH FRIENDS | IT'S A FUNNY STORY ACTUALLY |

Most of our get-togethers have ended with (circle those that apply)

| TEARS OF LAUGHTER | EMPTY BANK ACCOUNTS | TRIPS TO THE E.R | BLACKOUTS |

Remember that time when we
_____
_____

My birthday wish for you is _____
_____

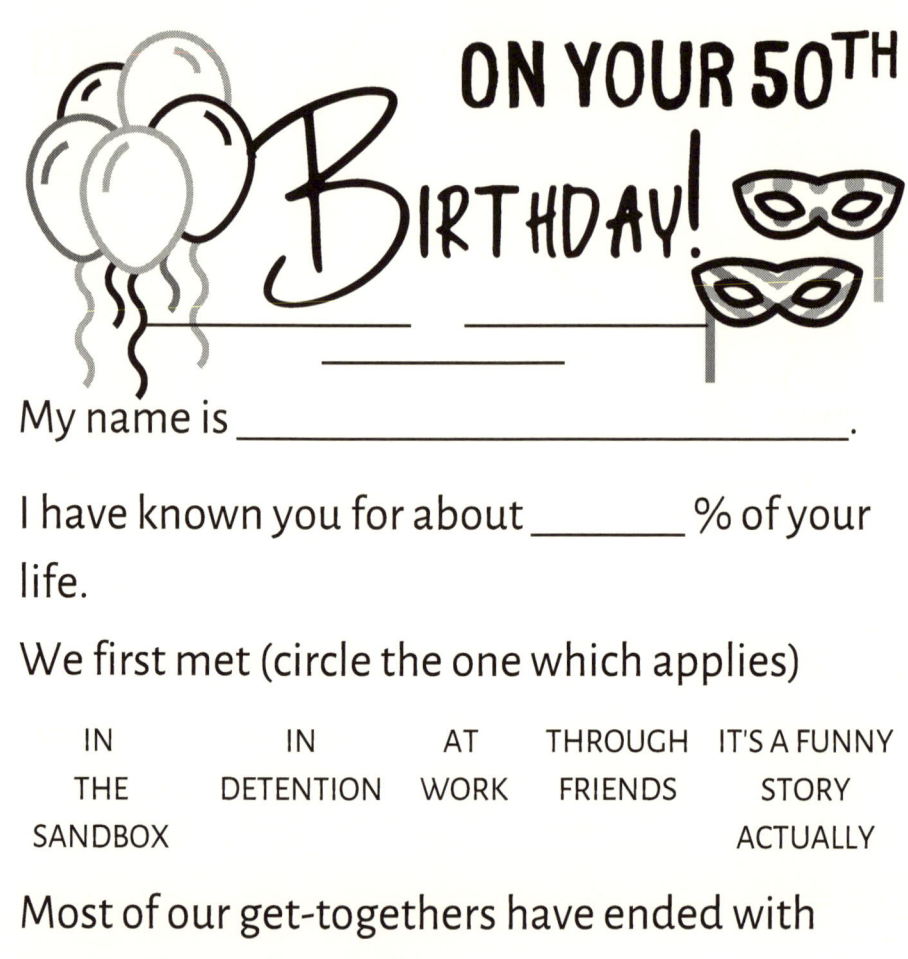

ON YOUR 50TH Birthday!

My name is _____.

I have known you for about _____ % of your life.

We first met (circle the one which applies)

| IN THE SANDBOX | IN DETENTION | AT WORK | THROUGH FRIENDS | IT'S A FUNNY STORY ACTUALLY |

Most of our get-togethers have ended with (circle those that apply)

| TEARS OF LAUGHTER | EMPTY BANK ACCOUNTS | TRIPS TO THE E.R | BLACKOUTS |

Remember that time when we

_____

_____

My birthday wish for you is _____

_____.

ON YOUR 50TH Birthday!

My name is _____.

I have known you for about _____ % of your life.

We first met (circle the one which applies)

| IN THE SANDBOX | IN DETENTION | AT WORK | THROUGH FRIENDS | IT'S A FUNNY STORY ACTUALLY |

Most of our get-togethers have ended with (circle those that apply)

| TEARS OF LAUGHTER | EMPTY BANK ACCOUNTS | TRIPS TO THE E.R | BLACKOUTS |

Remember that time when we

_____

_____

My birthday wish for you is _____

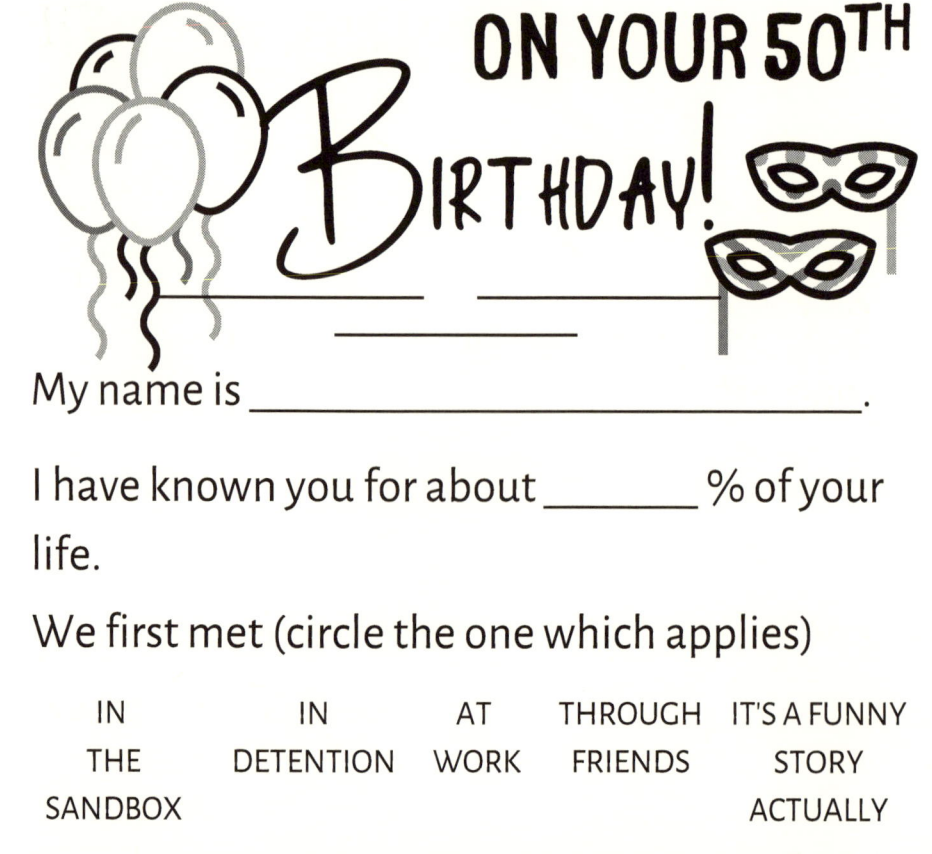

_____

ON YOUR 50TH BIRTHDAY!

My name is _____.

I have known you for about _____ % of your life.

We first met (circle the one which applies)

| IN THE SANDBOX | IN DETENTION | AT WORK | THROUGH FRIENDS | IT'S A FUNNY STORY ACTUALLY |

Most of our get-togethers have ended with (circle those that apply)

| TEARS OF LAUGHTER | EMPTY BANK ACCOUNTS | TRIPS TO THE E.R | BLACKOUTS |

Remember that time when we
_____
_____

My birthday wish for you is _____
_____.

ON YOUR 50TH Birthday!

_____ _____
  _____

My name is _____.

I have known you for about _____ % of your life.

We first met (circle the one which applies)

| IN THE SANDBOX | IN DETENTION | AT WORK | THROUGH FRIENDS | IT'S A FUNNY STORY ACTUALLY |

Most of our get-togethers have ended with (circle those that apply)

| TEARS OF LAUGHTER | EMPTY BANK ACCOUNTS | TRIPS TO THE E.R | BLACKOUTS |

Remember that time when we
_____
_____

My birthday wish for you is _____
_____

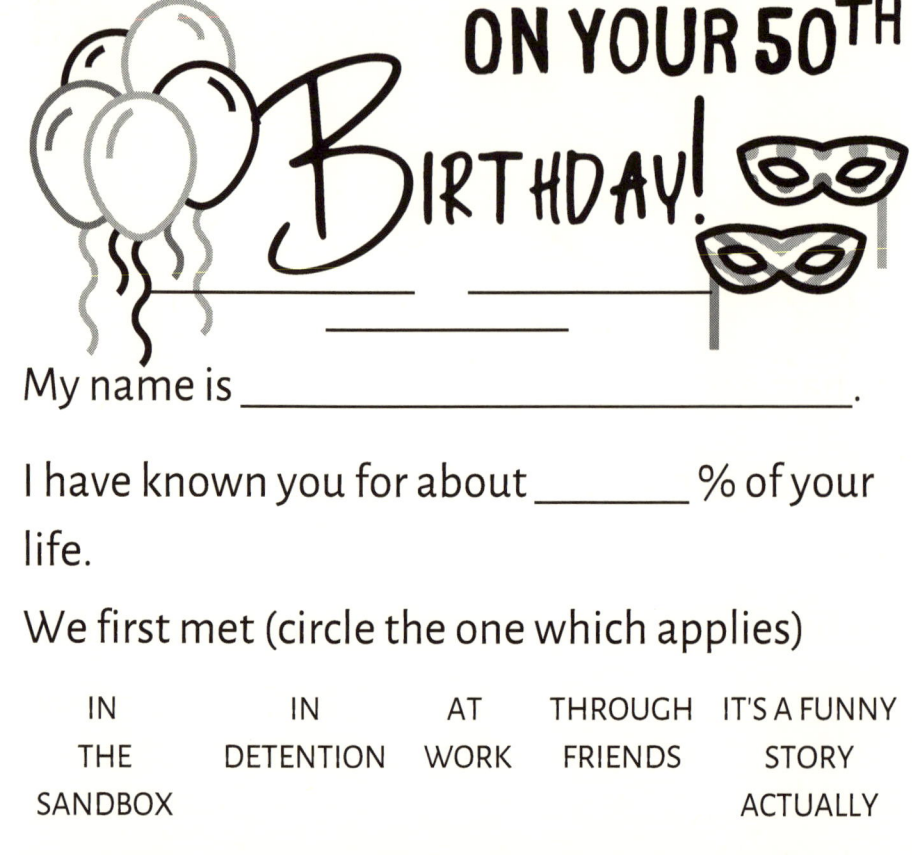

ON YOUR 50TH BIRTHDAY!

My name is _____.

I have known you for about _____ % of your life.

We first met (circle the one which applies)

| IN THE SANDBOX | IN DETENTION | AT WORK | THROUGH FRIENDS | IT'S A FUNNY STORY ACTUALLY |

Most of our get-togethers have ended with (circle those that apply)

| TEARS OF LAUGHTER | EMPTY BANK ACCOUNTS | TRIPS TO THE E.R | BLACKOUTS |

Remember that time when we
_____
_____

My birthday wish for you is _____
_____.

ON YOUR 50TH Birthday!

My name is _____.

I have known you for about _____ % of your life.

We first met (circle the one which applies)

| IN THE SANDBOX | IN DETENTION | AT WORK | THROUGH FRIENDS | IT'S A FUNNY STORY ACTUALLY |

Most of our get-togethers have ended with (circle those that apply)

| TEARS OF LAUGHTER | EMPTY BANK ACCOUNTS | TRIPS TO THE E.R | BLACKOUTS |

Remember that time when we

_____

_____

My birthday wish for you is _____

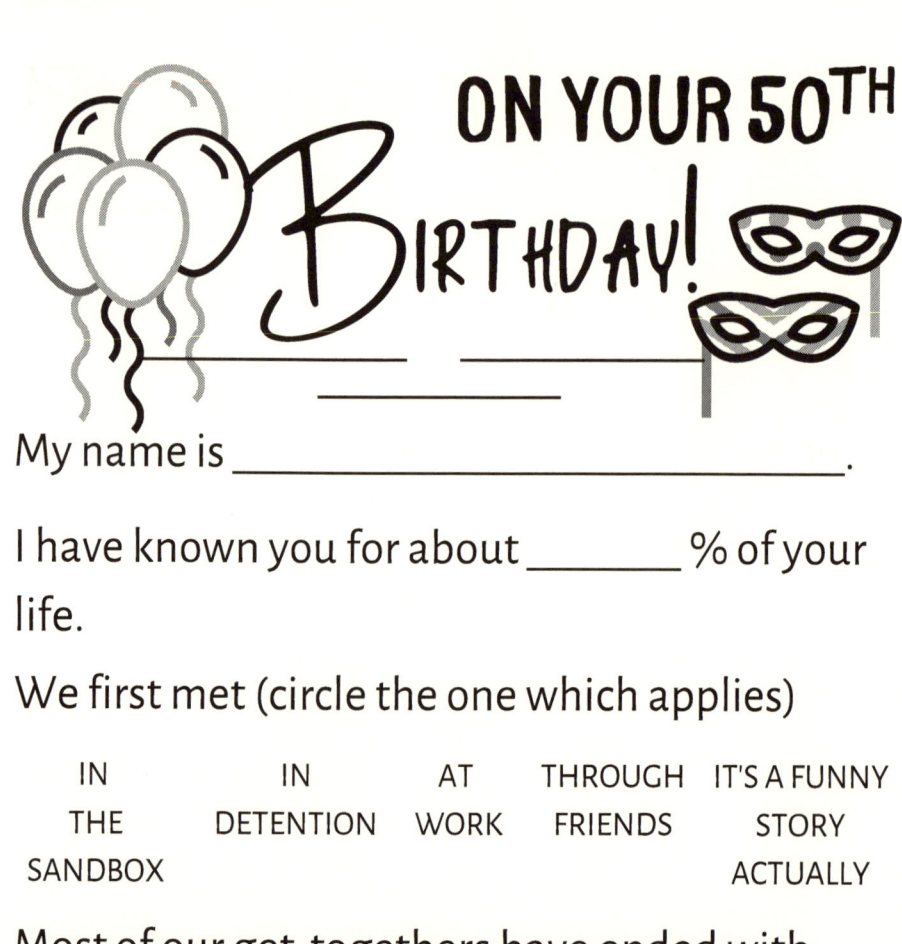

_____

ON YOUR 50TH Birthday!

_____ _____

My name is _____.

I have known you for about _____ % of your life.

We first met (circle the one which applies)

| IN THE SANDBOX | IN DETENTION | AT WORK | THROUGH FRIENDS | IT'S A FUNNY STORY ACTUALLY |

Most of our get-togethers have ended with (circle those that apply)

| TEARS OF LAUGHTER | EMPTY BANK ACCOUNTS | TRIPS TO THE E.R | BLACKOUTS |

Remember that time when we

_____

_____

My birthday wish for you is _____

_____.

ON YOUR 50TH Birthday!

My name is _____.

I have known you for about _____ % of your life.

We first met (circle the one which applies)

    IN THE SANDBOX   IN DETENTION   AT WORK   THROUGH FRIENDS   IT'S A FUNNY STORY ACTUALLY

Most of our get-togethers have ended with (circle those that apply)

    TEARS OF LAUGHTER   EMPTY BANK ACCOUNTS   TRIPS TO THE E.R   BLACKOUTS

Remember that time when we

_____

_____

My birthday wish for you is _____

_____.

ON YOUR 50TH BIRTHDAY!

My name is _____.

I have known you for about _____ % of your life.

We first met (circle the one which applies)

| IN THE SANDBOX | IN DETENTION | AT WORK | THROUGH FRIENDS | IT'S A FUNNY STORY ACTUALLY |

Most of our get-togethers have ended with (circle those that apply)

| TEARS OF LAUGHTER | EMPTY BANK ACCOUNTS | TRIPS TO THE E.R | BLACKOUTS |

Remember that time when we
_____
_____

My birthday wish for you is _____
_____.

Made in the USA
Las Vegas, NV
22 January 2022